For Dad – oceans of love – C.H.

For Podrick, Pawel, Luther and Otis,
the four-legged explorers who kept me
company on this adventure! – B.W.

BLOOMSBURY CHILDREN'S BOOKS
Bloomsbury Publishing Plc
50 Bedford Square, London, WC1B 3DP, UK

BLOOMSBURY, BLOOMSBURY CHILDREN'S BOOKS and the Diana logo are trademarks of Bloomsbury Publishing Plc
First published in Great Britain by Bloomsbury Publishing Plc

ISBN 978 1 5266 0364 7 (HB)
ISBN 978 1 5266 0363 0 (PB)
ISBN 978 1 5266 0362 3 (eBook)

1 3 5 7 9 10 8 6 4 2

Printed and bound in China by Leo Paper Products, Heshan, Guangdong
All papers used by Bloomsbury Publishing Plc are natural, recyclable products from wood grown in well managed forests.
The manufacturing processes conform to the environmental regulations of the country of origin.

To find out more about our authors and books visit www.bloomsbury.com and sign up for our newsletters

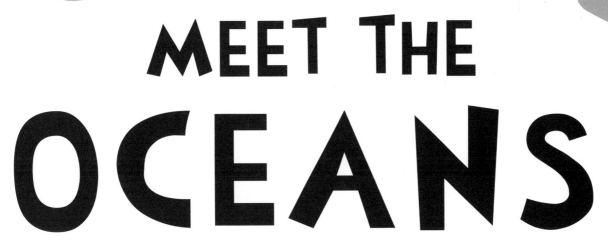

MEET THE OCEANS

Caryl Hart

Illustrated by **Bethan Woollvin**

BLOOMSBURY
CHILDREN'S BOOKS
LONDON   OXFORD   NEW YORK   NEW DELHI   SYDNEY

Have you ever been down to the seaside
where the waves splash and CRASH to and fro?
Or peeped over the edge of a jetty
at the sea life that wriggles below?

Well, you might be surprised to discover
that so much of our planet is sea
and, within it, live millions of creatures
that are beautiful, strange, wild and free.

So . . .

Let's dive through a world full of mystery
and go visit the **oceans** and **seas**
on a **submarine** epic adventure . . .

Brrrr! I'm the cold **ARCTIC OCEAN**.
I'm **f-freezing** – and, look, so are you!
In my waters swim **narwhals** and **walrus**,
and these friendly **beluga whales** too!

Giant **jellyfish** float near my surface,
furry **polar bears** pad on my ice.
and I might be the world's SMALLEST ocean –
but I think being little's quite nice.

I'm the breezy **ATLANTIC**, you've found me –
a **VAST** ocean of winds and of waves.
And d'you know? I have **mountains** below me,
and hundreds of undersea **caves**.

Sparkling diamonds hide down in my sea bed,
silver **swordfish** and **salmon** swim free.
And while swishing around in the sea grass,
you might spot the odd wild **manatee**!

Hey there, let's chill out, put your feet up.
I'm the warm **CARIBBEAN SEA**. Yay!
I have thousands of tropical islands –
so come floating with me – what d'you say?

We'll meet **angelfish**, **trunkfish** and **porkfish**.
I have **blue tangs** and **jawfish** and rays.
But don't try to count all my starfish and crabs –
you'll be UNDER the water for **days**!

Ahoy there! Yo! I'm the **PACIFIC**.
I'm the world's BIGGEST ocean – yippee!
But I'm facing a bit of a **problem**,
is there any chance YOU could help me?

You see, **millions** of pieces of **plastic**
have been making my **oceans** feel sick.
Please tell everyone, "Don't dump your rubbish!"
So my **sea life** can get better quick.

I'm the **SOUTH CHINA SEA** – woah! Be careful.
There are ships everywhere – quick, make way!
And, look, deep in my **BUSTLING** waters
countless creatures all beaver away.

Seabirds jostle and *swoop* round above me,
then dive down like sharp darts to catch food.
It's a wild, hectic life and I LOVE it,
and that's why I'm in such a great mood!

I'm the blue **CoRAL SEA**,
glad you've found me!
My Great Barrier Reef is so cool.
You can see it from space, it's so MASSIVE –
like a GLITTERING string of sea jewels.

I'm a haven for lobsters and sea snakes;
you'll meet three hundred species of shark.
Many thousands of fish come to feed here –
I'm an undersea animal ark!

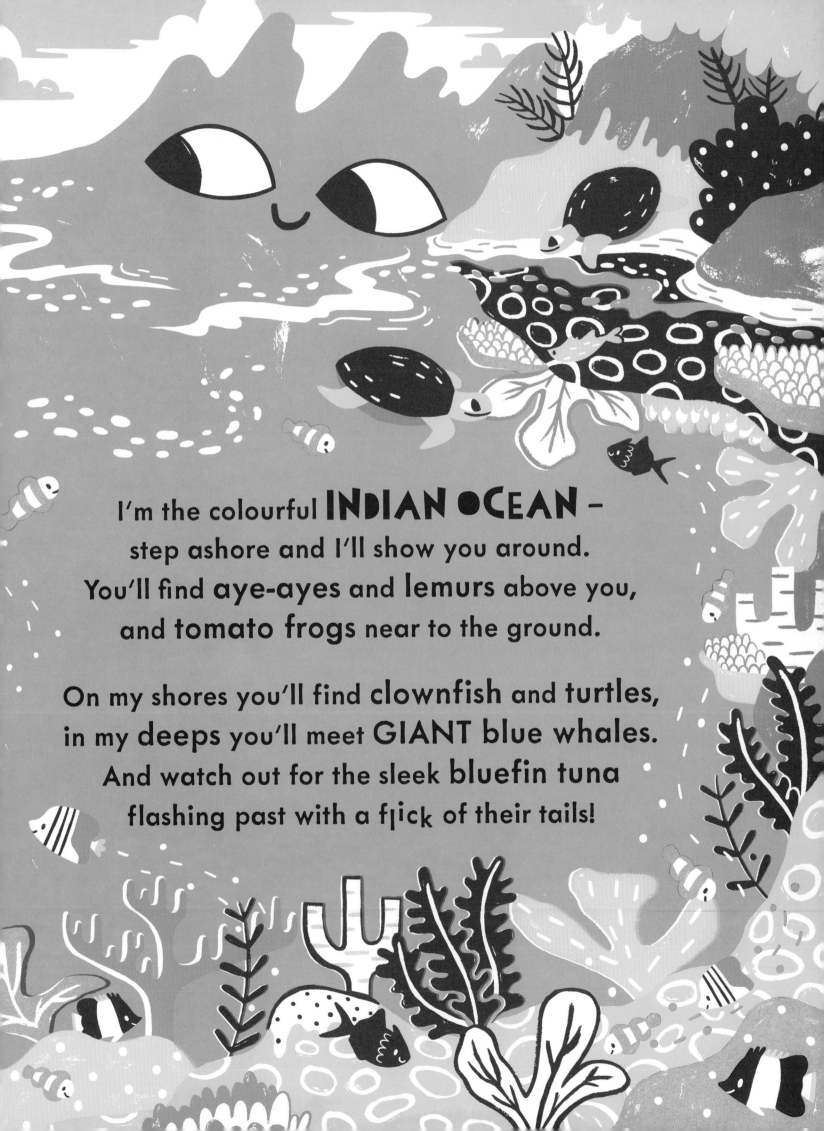

I'm the colourful **INDIAN OCEAN** –
step ashore and I'll show you around.
You'll find **aye-ayes** and **lemurs** above you,
and **tomato frogs** near to the ground.

On my shores you'll find **clownfish** and **turtles**,
in my deeps you'll meet **GIANT** blue whales.
And watch out for the sleek **bluefin tuna**
flashing past with a flick of their tails!

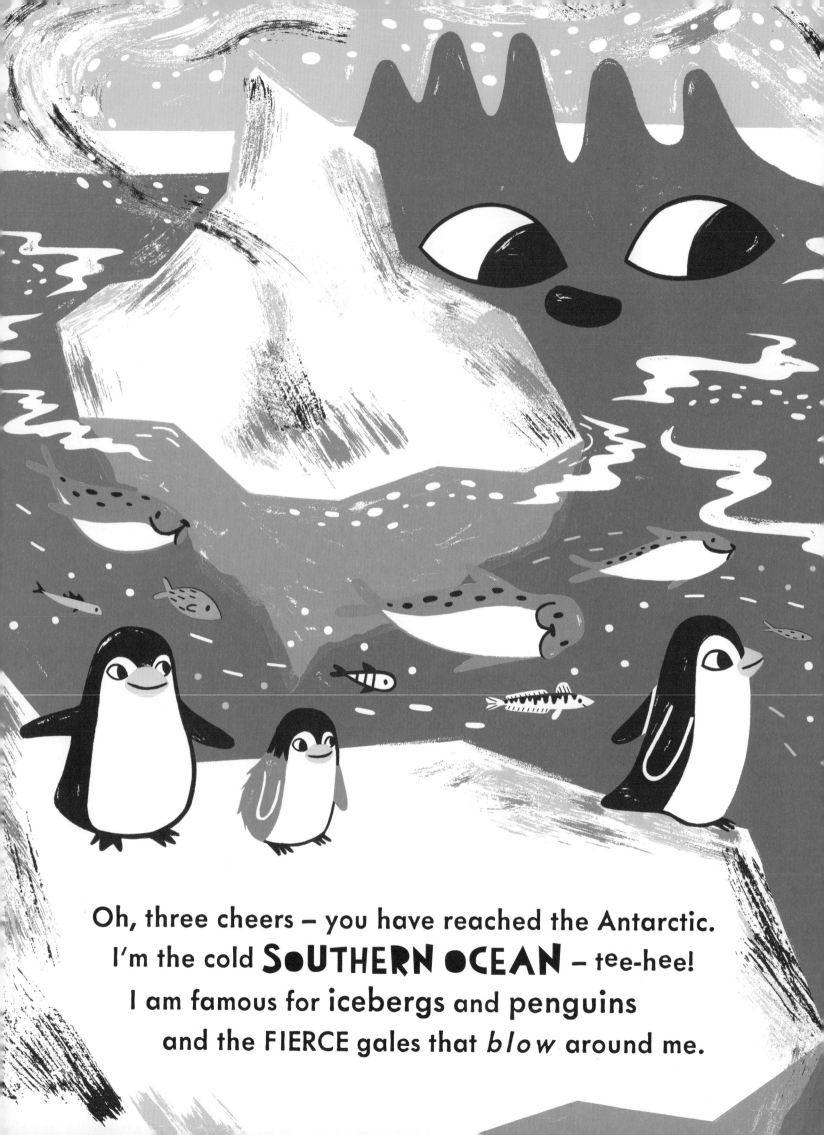

Oh, three cheers — you have reached the Antarctic.
I'm the cold **SOUTHERN OCEAN** — tee-hee!
I am famous for icebergs and penguins
and the FIERCE gales that *blow* around me.

At my **ports** are some real special buildings.
They're called **research** stations, you know.
They're where scientists study all sorts of cool things
such as **climate change**, wildlife and **snow**!

Hey, how lovely you've come for a visit.
I'm the **MEDITERRANEAN SEA!**
LOADS of tourists come here – and no wonder.
I'm as **gorgeous** and great as can be.

We've had such an AMAZING adventure
and made so many **friends** on the way,
but at last we will have to head **homewards**,
though I'm sure we'll come back here one day.

So the next time you sit in your bathtub,
    please remember the **oceans** and **seas**.
And the wonderful **creatures** who live there –
    and make sure you look after them please.

ARCTIC OCEAN

MEDITERRANEAN SEA

SOUTH CHINA SEA

INDIAN OCEAN

CORAL SEA

SOUTHERN OCEAN